HISTORIC CIVILIZATIONS

ANCIENT ROME

Colin Hynson

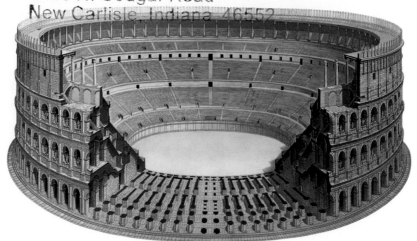

GARETH**STEVENS**
GS
PUBLISHING
A World Almanac Education Group Company

How to use this book

Each topic in this book is clearly labeled and contains all these components:

Topic heading

Introduction to the topic

Subtopic 1 gives information about one aspect of the topic.

Words that are in the topic glossary are bolded the first time they appear on the page.

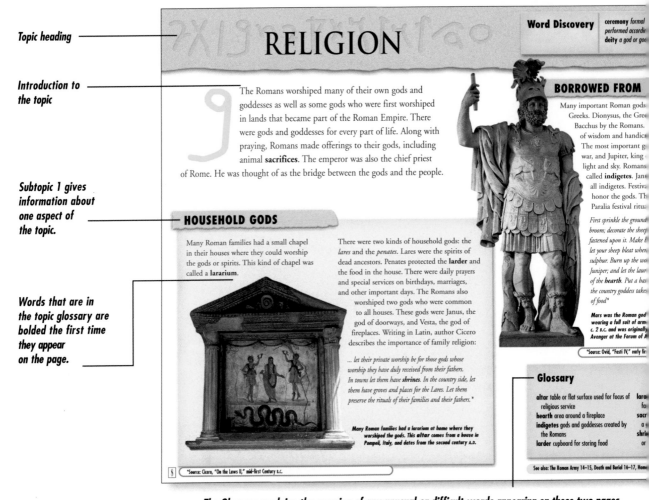

RELIGION

The Romans worshiped many of their own gods and goddesses as well as some gods who were first worshiped in lands that became part of the Roman Empire. There were gods and goddesses for every part of life. Along with praying, Romans made offerings to their gods, including animal **sacrifices**. The emperor was also the chief priest of Rome. He was thought of as the bridge between the gods and the people.

HOUSEHOLD GODS

Many Roman families had a small chapel in their houses where they could worship the gods or spirits. This kind of chapel was called a **lararium**.

There were two kinds of household gods: the *lares* and the *penates*. Lares were the spirits of dead ancestors. Penates protected the **larder** and the food in the house. There were daily prayers and special services on birthdays, marriages, and other important days. The Romans also worshiped two gods who were common to all houses. These gods were Janus, the god of doorways, and Vesta, the god of fireplaces. Writing in Latin, author Cicero describes the importance of family religion:

... let their private worship be for those gods whose worship they have duly received from their fathers. In towns let them have **shrines**. *In the country side, let them have groves and places for the Lares. Let them preserve the rituals of their families and their fathers.**

Many Roman families had a lararium at home where they worshiped the gods. This **altar** comes from a house in Pompeii, Italy, and dates from the second century A.D.

8 *Source: Cicero, "On the Laws II," mid-first Century B.C.*

Word Discovery ceremony formal performed accordir deity a god or goe

BORROWED FROM

Many important Roman gods Greeks. Dionysus, the Gree Bacchus by the Romans. of wisdom and handic The most important g war, and Jupiter, king light and sky. Romans called **indigetes**. Jan all indigetes. Festiva honor the gods. Th Paralia festival ritua

*First sprinkle the groun. broom; decorate the shee fastened upon it. Make t let your sheep bleat wher sulphur. Burn up the wo Juniper; and let the laur of the **hearth**. Put a bas the country goddess takes of food**

Mars was the Roman god wearing a full suit of arm c. 2 B.C. and was originally Avenger at the Forum of A

Source: Ovid, "Fasti IV," early fir

Glossary

altar table or flat surface used for focus of religious service
hearth area around a fireplace
indigetes gods and goddesses created by the Romans
larder cupboard for storing food

lara
fau
sacr
a
shri
or

See also: The Roman Army 14–15, Death and Burial 16–17, Hom

The Glossary explains the meaning of any unusual or difficult words appearing on these two pages.

Please visit our web site at: **www.garethstevens.com**
For a free color catalog describing Gareth Stevens Publishing's list of high-quality books and multimedia programs, call **1-800-542-2595** (USA) or **1-800-387-3178** (Canada). **Gareth Stevens Publishing's fax: (414) 332-3567.**

Library of Congress Cataloging-in-Publication Data

Hynson, Colin.
   Ancient Rome / Colin Hynson.
      p. cm. — (Historic civilizations)
   Includes index.
   ISBN 0-8368-4200-6 (lib. bdg.)
   1. Rome—Civilization—Juvenile literature. 2. Rome—Social life and customs—Juvenile literature. I. Title. II. Series.
DG78.H95 2004
937—dc22   2004045302

This North American edition first published in 2005 by
Gareth Stevens Publishing
A World Almanac Education Group Company
330 West Olive Street, Suite 100
Milwaukee, Wisconsin 53212 USA

This U.S. edition copyright © 2005 by Gareth Stevens, Inc. Original edition copyright © 2004 ticktock Entertainment Ltd. First published in Great Britain in 2004 as *Your Ancient Rome Homework Helper* by ticktock Media Ltd., Unit 2, Orchard Business Centre, North Farm Road, Tunbridge Wells, Kent TN23XF, UK.

The publishers wish to thank Isabella Sandwell and Egan-Reid Ltd. for their research and consulting expertise in the making of this book.

Gareth Stevens editor: Barbara Kiely Miller
Gareth Stevens cover design: Steve Schraenkler

Printed in the United States of America

1 2 3 4 5 6 7 8 9 08 07 06 05 04

Subtopic 2 gives information about another aspect of the topic.

The Case Study is a closer look at a famous person, artifact, or building that relates to the topic.

Discover other words that relate to the topic.

Each photo or illustration is described and discussed in the accompanying text.

Captions clearly explain what is in the picture.

At the bottom of some sections, a reference bar tells where the information has come from.

Other pages in the book that relate to what you have read in this topic are listed here.

A reference bar marked with an asterisk (*) gives the source of the quotations in the text.

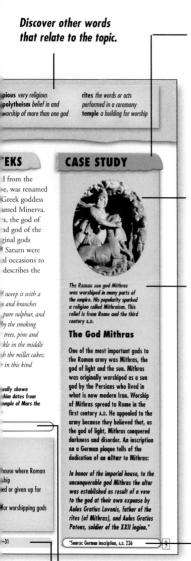

pious *very religious*
polytheism *belief in and worship of more than one god*

rites *the words or acts performed in a ceremony*
temple *a building for worship*

'EKS

d from the
e, was renamed
Greek goddess
amed Minerva.
s, the god of
d god of the
ginal gods
Saturn were
al occasions to
describes the

sweep it with a
and branches
pure sulphur, and
by the smoking
trees, pine and
kle in the middle
h the millet cakes;
in this kind

ually shown
him dates from
mple of Mars the

house where Roman
ship
ed or given up for

for worshipping gods

—31

CASE STUDY

The Roman sun god Mithras was worshiped in many parts of the empire. His popularity sparked a religion called Mithraism. This relief is from Rome and the third century A.D.

The God Mithras

One of the most important gods to the Roman army was Mithras, the god of light and the sun. Mithras was originally worshiped as a sun god by the Persians who lived in what is now modern Iran. Worship of Mithras spread to Rome in the first century A.D. He appealed to the army because they believed that, as the god of light, Mithras conquered darkness and disorder. An inscription on a German plaque tells of the dedication of an altar to Mithras:

In honor of the imperial house, to the unconquerable god Mithras the altar was established as result of a vow to the god at their own expense by Aulus Gratius Luvonis, father of the rites (of Mithras), and Aulus Gratius Potens, soldier of the XXII legion.*

*Source: German inscription, A.D. 236

Keyword Contents

CREATION OF THE ROMAN EMPIRE

The Italian city of Rome was once ruled by kings. In 509 B.C., King Tarquin, "the Proud," was driven out of the city and Rome became a **republic**. Afterward, Rome began to overpower and rule its neighbors. The Roman **Empire** soon grew across Europe, North Africa, and Asia. Today, taking control of another country by force is usually seen as wrong, but the Romans believed they were bringing civilization to people they considered **barbarians**.

THE REACH OF THE ROMAN EMPIRE

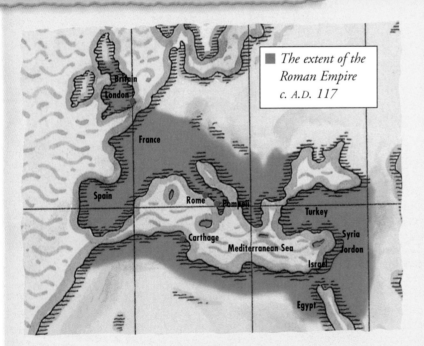

The extent of the Roman Empire c. A.D. 117

This map shows the Roman Empire at its height under Emperor Trajan, in the second century A.D.

Places taken over by the Roman Empire included parts of present-day Spain in 197 B.C. and France, Turkey, Syria, Egypt, Israel, and Jordan in the first century B.C. In its later years, the empire had **corruption** and military problems. Roman writers such as Cassius Dio and Herodian described them:

*What was the use of destroying barbarians, when the killing in Rome itself and the provinces subject to her was on a larger scale? What was the use of seizing **booty** from the enemy, only to be stripped naked oneself and see one's relatives deprived of their property? An invitation had been given to informers to do their **dastardly** work with complete license.**

Soon after becoming a republic, Rome took control of the area that is modern-day Italy and the other territories that surrounded the Mediterranean Sea. A few hundred years later, the Romans also began to **conquer** other lands.

*Source: Herodian, "History VII.iii.1," third century A.D.

Word Discovery

civilization *high level of cultural development*

deposed *removed from power*

monarch *king or queen*

occupy *take up or control a place, sometimes by force*

prosper *succeed financially*

seized *taken by force*

subdue *bring under control*

THE FOUNDING OF THE ROMAN EMPIRE

brothers Romulus and Remus. They were the sons of Mars, the Roman god of war. When they were babies, their uncle put them into the Tiber River to drown. A wolf rescued and nursed them. When the brothers grew up, they killed their uncle and started the city of Rome. Roman author Cicero wrote about Rome's beginnings:

*Consequently it seems to me that Romulus must at the very beginning have had a **divine intimation** that the city would one day be the seat and hearthstone of a mighty empire; for scarcely could a city placed upon any other site in Italy have more easily maintained our present widespread **dominion**.* *

This carving from the second century A.D. shows legendary brothers Romulus and Remus with the wolf that raised them.

According to Roman legend, Rome was **founded** in 753 B.C. by twin

*Source: Cicero, "Republic V," mid-first century B.C.

Glossary

booty treasure taken over in a war

barbarians people with an inferior culture

conquer to overcome by force or strategy

corruption improper actions done in return for money or personal gain

dastardly cruel or cowardly

divine intimation a vision from God

dominion authority over land or people

empire lands ruled over by a single country, ruler, or king

founded built or started something

republic a country whose citizens elect a small group to govern by law

sovereignty supreme power or authority

See also: Rulers and Ruled 6–7, Travel and Trade 12–13, Roman Army 14–15, Buildings and Engineering 18–19

CASE STUDY

Emperor Claudius is depicted in this first century A.D. bronze bust.

Conquering Britain

The Roman empire began expanding into Britain in 55 B.C. when ruler Julius Caesar landed his army on the coast of Kent. After a second attempt the next year, almost one hundred years passed before the Romans invaded Britain again. They attacked in the spring of A.D. 43. Emperor Claudius arrived in Britain that autumn and led his troops into Colchester. Thirty-five years later, all but northern Britain had been conquered and become part of the Roman Empire. An inscription from Rome marks Claudius' victory in Britain and praises him because:

*... he received the surrender of eleven kings of Britain conquered without reverse and because he was the first to subject to the **sovereignty** of the Roman people barbarian tribes across the ocean.* *

*Source: "Corpus Inscriptionum Latinarum vol VI no. 920" mid-first century A.D.

RULERS AND RULED

The emperor was positioned at the top of Roman society. Next in rank were **consuls**, who managed the **Senate** and the Roman armies, and **senators**, who made the laws. People in the empire were divided into citizens and non-citizens. Citizens had certain rights and privileges that were denied to non-citizens. Slaves were at the bottom of Roman society and had no rights at all.

KEEPING THE LAW

In 451 and 450 B.C., the Twelve Tables were created. These were the first written records of Roman laws, and they were written on twelve wood tablets. They provided the basis for law and order over the next one thousand years. If anyone was suspected of breaking the law they had to face the local judge or **praetor**.

The praetors were served and accompanied by two or more lictors. A lictor would carry the **fasces** on his shoulder. The fasces was an axe tied inside a bundle of rods. It symbolized the praetor's right to punish and put to death anyone found guilty of a crime. The most powerful praetors were the governors of the various parts of the Roman Empire. Only the emperor was more powerful than these praetors. Many writers during that time described Roman officials as being corrupt. Poet Juvenal suggested this corruption in a passage from one of his *Satires*:

*When at last the province to which you have long looked forward receives you as governor, put a **rein** and **curb** on your anger, and on your greed; take some pity on the poor **provincials**, keep in mind what the law prescribes, what the senate lies down.* *

This bronze figurine of a lictor carrying the fasces is from c. 20 B.C. to A.D. 20.

*Source: Juvenal, "Satire 8.88-91," late-first to early-second century B.C.

Word Discovery

assassinated *killed*
corruption *dishonest or illegal behavior*

democracy *country where citizens have final power*
magistrate *government*

official or judge
ruthless *having no pity*
stable *not easily changed*

ROME'S LAW MAKERS

The Senate was a governing group of Romans who were elected by and who represented the citizens of Rome. It was responsible for making laws. When Rome was still a republic, the Senate was the most important organization in the empire. Once the emperors began to rule, the senate was reduced in power to just advising the emperor and serving as a court of law.

Writers such as Tacitus noted the way in which the senators flattered the emperors. One emperor, Tiberius, even described

Roman senators are shown in this detail from an Italian coffin made in A.D. 270.

them as "men fit to be slaves,"* meaning that senators groveled before the emperors in the same way slaves served their masters.

*Source: Tacitus, "Annals III.64," late-first century A.D.

CASE STUDY

This marble statue of Emperor Augustus was made about 63 B.C. and is from Vellentri, Italy.

The First Emperor

The Roman Empire was not always ruled by emperors. For 536 years, it was a republic and governed by generals who fought each other for control of Rome. General Julius Caesar ruled for many years but was murdered in 44 B.C. After his death, his adopted son, Augustus, restored order and was declared the first Emperor of Rome in 27 B.C. He ruled until his death in A.D. 14. Augustus was thought of as a wise ruler who advanced the empire and improved the lives of its people. He recorded his many achievements in a temple inscription called "Res Gestae." His account describes:

*The achievements of the divine Augustus by which he brought the world under the empire of the Roman people and the expenses which he bore for the state and people of Rome.**

*Source: Augustus, "Res Gestae," end-first century B.C.

Glossary

consuls the top Roman magistrates
curb hold back
fasces a symbol of Roman law and authority
praetor a Roman magistrate
provincials people who live in smaller parts of a country or empire

rein control or stop
satires literary work ridiculing human behavior or weaknesses
Senate group of elected government officials who make laws
senators people elected by citizens to join the Senate

See also: Creation of the Empire 4–5, Language and Writing 10–11, The Roman Army 14–15, Gladiators 20–21

RELIGION

The Romans worshiped many of their own gods and goddesses as well as some gods who were first worshiped in lands that became part of the Roman Empire. There were gods and goddesses for every part of life. Along with praying, Romans made offerings to their gods, including animal **sacrifices**. The emperor was also the chief priest of Rome. He was thought of as the bridge between the gods and the people.

HOUSEHOLD GODS

Many Roman families had a small chapel in their houses where they could worship the gods or spirits. This kind of chapel was called a **lararium**.

There were two kinds of household gods: the *lares* and the *penates*. Lares were the spirits of dead ancestors. Penates protected the **larder** and the food in the house. There were daily prayers and special services on birthdays, marriages, and other important days. The Romans also worshiped two gods who were common to all houses. These gods were Janus, the god of doorways, and Vesta, the god of fireplaces. Writing in Latin, author Cicero describes the importance of family religion:

*... let their private worship be for those gods whose worship they have duly received from their fathers. In towns let them have **shrines**. In the country side, let them have groves and places for the Lares. Let them preserve the rituals of their families and their fathers.**

Many Roman families had a lararium at home where they worshiped the gods. This altar comes from a house in Pompeii, Italy, and dates from the second century A.D.

*Source: Cicero, "On the Laws II," mid-first Century B.C.

Word Discovery

ceremony *formal event performed according to ritual*
deity *a god or goddess*

pious *very religious*
polytheism *belief in and worship of more than one god*

rites *the words or acts performed in a ceremony*
temple *a building for worship*

BORROWED FROM THE GREEKS

Many important Roman gods were adopted from the Greeks. Dionysus, the Greek god of wine, was renamed Bacchus by the Romans. Athena, the Greek goddess of wisdom and handicrafts, was renamed Minerva. The most important gods were Mars, the god of war, and Jupiter, king of the gods and god of the light and sky. Romans also had original gods called **indigetes**. Janus, Vesta, and Saturn were all indigetes. Festivals were special occasions to honor the gods. The poet Ovid describes the Paralia festival rituals:

*First sprinkle the ground with water and sweep it with a broom; decorate the sheep-pen with leaves and branches fastened upon it. Make blue smoke from pure sulphur, and let your sheep bleat when she is touched by the smoking sulphur. Burn up the wood of male olive trees, pine and Juniper; and let the laurel singe and crackle in the middle of the **hearth**. Put a basket of millet with the millet cakes; the country goddess takes special pleasure in this kind of food.**

Mars was the Roman god of war and is usually shown wearing a full suit of armor. This statue of him dates from c. 2 B.C. and was originally located at the Temple of Mars the Avenger at the Forum of Augustus in Rome.

*Source: Ovid, "Fasti IV," early first century B.C.

Glossary

altar table or flat surface used for focus of religious service
hearth area around a fireplace
indigetes gods and goddesses created by the Romans
larder cupboard for storing food

lararium place in a house where Roman families would worship
sacrifices things killed or given up for a god
shrines holy places for worshipping gods or a sacred person

See also: The Roman Army 14–15, Death and Burial 16–17, Homes 28–29, Leisure 30–31

CASE STUDY

The Roman sun god Mithras was worshiped in many parts of the empire. His popularity sparked a religion called Mithraism. This relief is from Rome and the third century A.D.

The God Mithras

One of the most important gods to the Roman army was Mithras, the god of light and the sun. Mithras was originally worshiped as a sun god by the Persians who lived in what is now modern Iran. Worship of Mithras spread to Rome in the first century A.D. He appealed to the army because they believed that, as the god of light, Mithras conquered darkness and disorder. An inscription on a German plaque tells of the dedication of an **altar** to Mithras:

In honor of the imperial house, to the unconquerable god Mithras the altar was established as result of a vow to the god at their own expense by Aulus Gratius Luvenis, father of the rites (of Mithras), and Aulus Gratius Potens, soldier of the XXII legion.*

*Source: German inscription, A.D. 236

LANGUAGE AND WRITING

A Roman writer named Cicero believed that better communication within the Roman Empire would help make its people more **civilized**. There were many different languages across the empire. To help with communication, **Latin** was used in the west of the empire and Greek in the east. These languages were used for international trade and government. For many of the **territories** conquered by the Romans this was the first time that writing was used as a form of communication.

PAPER AND PENS

Roman writing tools included a wax tablet with two wooden leaves that folded together.

Liquid wax was poured onto the tablet and allowed to harden. The point of a **stylus** was used like a pen to scratch words into the wax. At the other end of the stylus was a flat end that was used like an eraser, smoothing the wax surface to erase any writing to be changed. **Papyrus** was a kind of paper that was made from reeds. It originally came from Egypt. Papyrus was expensive to make and was only used for important documents like **contracts**. Romans wrote on papyrus with a pen that would have been made from a reed and with ink that was a mixture of soot and olive oil. Roman naturalist Pliny the Elder describes the making of paper from papyrus:

... paper is made from the papyrus plant by separating it with a needle point into very thin strips as broad as possible. *

Most writing was done with a stylus and a wooden wax tablet like this. The inkwell once held ink used for writing on papyrus.

*Source: Pliny, "Natural History, XIII," early-first century A.D.

ROMAN ALPHABET

The letters shown here (*left*) are carved into the base of Trajan's Column in Rome. Carvings and writing from the time of the Roman Empire show that there were only 22 letters in the Roman alphabet and that all of them were capital letters. The Romans did not have the letters W and Y. They also used one letter for I and J and one for U and V. The style of Roman lettering is still used by printers today. The Romans also used letters to write numbers: I for 1, V for 5, X for 10, L for 50, C for 100, D for 500, and M for 1000. Roman **numerals** are still used today, often on clocks and watches.

These Roman letters are carved on Trajan's Column. It was built in Rome in A.D. 113 by Emperor Trajan as a monument to his military conquests.

CASE STUDY

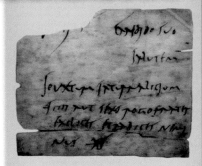

The Vindolanda Tablets are letters from people living in northern England in the first and second centuries A.D.

Writing letters

The Vindolanda Tablets give a glimpse into the lives of ordinary people who lived at the Roman fort at Vindolanda in northern England. The tablets are made of thinly cut slivers of wood. Letters were written on one side. The wood was then folded in half and the address written on the back. One of the first tablets to be translated says:

I have sent you ... pairs of socks from Sattua, two pairs of sandals and two pairs of underpants ... I hope that you live in the greatest good fortune.*

Glossary

contracts agreements between people or groups, put into writing

civilized having advanced cultural skills, including writing

Latin the official language of ancient Rome

numerals symbols for numbers

papyrus a kind of paper made from the papyrus plant

stylus tool for writing or marking

territories lands ruled by a single country, state, or person

See also: Rulers and Ruled 6–7, Travel and Trade 12–13, Buildings and Engineering 18–19

*Source: Vindolanda Tablet 346, 1st–2nd Century A.D.

TRAVEL AND TRADE

The wealth of the Roman Empire helped many areas of the empire to develop goods for **trading**. The records left by Roman **merchants** show that the eastern part of the empire produced wine, fruit, and silk; North Africa produced grain; and Gaul (present-day France) and Spain made olive oil and wine. The Roman army built many roads, which allowed goods to travel quickly and easily across the empire. Merchants also moved their goods by ship across the Mediterranean Sea.

ROADS OF THE ROMAN EMPIRE

This road in Pompeii, Italy, shows the straight lines that were common in Roman road building.

Roman roads are famous for being extremely straight. Emperors boasted about and wanted to be remembered for the straight roads that were built during the time of their rule. An inscription found next to a road from the reign of Emperor Trajan illustrates this:

*The Emperor Caesar Nerva Trajan Augustus Germanicus, son of the **deified** Nerva, pontifex maximus, holding the **tribunician** power for the fourth year, father of his country, consul three times, built this road by cutting through mountains and **eliminating** curves.* *

Roman roads were also built to be unusually strong. Their lasting strength is proven by the fact that many Roman roads still exist, although they are now under modern road surfaces. Ermine Street, which ran between the cities of London and York, is now part of England's highway system.

*Source: "Corpus Inscriptionum Latinarum vol III no. 8," c. A.D. 98-117

Word Discovery

calculate *find the answer by using mathematics*
commemorate *honor the*

memory of a person or event
expedition *journey*
industry *business*

nautical *sailing*
quantity *amount or number*

TRAVELING BY SEA

The Roman navy patrolled the seas of the empire, particularly the Mediterranean. The navy gave protection against pirates, who were a real problem for those who traded by sea. Merchant ships often sailed only during the summer months when the weather was safer as well. The Romans had no compasses, so they also made sure to always stay within sight of land. Writer Synesius wrote to his brother about sea travel:

*For in plain fact the big **rollers** still kept on, and the sea was at issue with itself. It does this when the wind falls, and the waves it has set going do not fall with it, but, still **retaining** in full force the **impulse** that started them, meet the onset of the gale, and to its front oppose their own. Well, when people are sailing in such circumstances, life hangs, as they say, by a slender thread.**

Sailing was dangerous in Roman times because of pirates and crude equipment. This relief of a sailing ship is from Italy and dates from the third century A.D.

*Source: Synesius, letter to his brother, c. late-third to early-fourth centuries A.D.

Glossary

deified worshiped as a god
eliminating getting rid of something
impulse sudden urge
retaining keeping
rollers large ocean or sea waves
steelyard part of a machine used for weighing

merchants people who trade for a living
trading buying and selling
tribunician Roman official chosen by the people to protect their interests
uncia The Romans' basic unit of weight

CASE STUDY

This bronze steelyard and lead weight was used in London in the first century A.D.

Weighing and Measuring

Trade became easier after the Romans standardized rules about measuring across the entire empire. Merchants from the furthest corners of the Roman Empire could then buy and sell from each other knowing that everyone was using the same system for measuring. The Romans' basic unit of weight was the **uncia** (the source of the word ounce). An uncia was equal to about 1 ounce (27 grams). The **steelyard** and weight (*above*) was one of the most common ways of weighing goods. The Romans sometimes used their denarius coin as a measure of weight. From c. 155 B.C. to A.D. 64 the denarius weighed 1/7 ounce (4 grams), as described by the writer, Celsus:

... in the ounce there is a weight of 7 denarii.*

*Source: Celsus, "On Medicine, V.17.1.C," mid-first century A.D.

See also: Writing 10-11, Buildings and Engineering 18–19, Food and Drink 24–25, Clothes and Jewelry 26–27

THE ROMAN ARMY

Life in the Roman Army was tough. Soldiers were killed for sleeping when they were supposed to be standing guard. As punishment for acts of **cowardice**, an army unit was **decimated**. Many men, however, still rushed to join the army. Not only did the army pay quite well, but it was a chance to learn new skills. After finishing their twenty to twenty-five years of service, soldiers were given land and money. These rewards came with rights and **privileges** that soldiers who were not Roman citizens would not have otherwise had.

WEAPONS

The ordinary soldier fought with a spear called a *pilum*, a dagger called a *pugio*, and a short sword called a *gladius*. He was also well protected by metal armor. These weapons made Roman soldiers very effective in battle. The Romans also used huge battering rams, stone-throwing machines, and a big crossbow that could fire bolts at enemy walls. A writer from the period describes the Roman weaponry:

The legion in practice is victorious because of the number of soldiers and the type of machines. First of all, it is equipped with hurling machines which no breastplate, no shield can withstand. For the practice is to have a ballista mounted on a carriage for each century, to each of which are assigned mules and a team of eleven men for loading and firing. *

Trajan's Column in Rome honors Emperor Trajan with scenes from the battles he fought in Dacia (modern Romania) between A.D. 101 and 106.

*Source: Vegetius, "Military Science II.23," c. early-fifth century A.D.

Word Discovery

artillery *large guns or other heavy weapons*
cease-fire *an armistice, or*

temporary halt in fighting
civilians *people who are not soldiers*

enlist *join the armed forces*
executed *killed as punishment*
infantry *an army's foot soldiers*

PEOPLE IN THE ARMY

The army was organized into legions. Each legion included about ten thousand men. An ordinary foot soldier was called a legionnaire. Ranking above a legionnaire was a centurion. A centurion had heavier armor. He also wore a helmet with a red plume, so he was easily recognized. Many soldiers were critical of their army superiors as illustrated in this account of a **mutiny** among the legions who were stationed at the empire's northern border in the first century A.D.:

Why should they obey like slaves a few centurions and fewer tribunes, when old men, and many who had lost limbs from wounds, were serving thirty and forty years?*

This Roman centurion is part of a second century relief from Turin, Italy.

*Source: Tacitus, "Annals I. xvii," late-first century B.C.

Glossary

cowardice lacking courage; demonstrating disgraceful fear
customarily most commonly
decimated when one out of ten soldiers was executed
entailing involving
forts army posts that may be surrounded with high walls and a ditch and have towers
mutiny rebellion against authority or superior officer
privileges special rights and favors
rampart a protective wall

CASE STUDY

This Roman fort was built between A.D. 120 and 138 in Cumbria, England.

Walls of Defense

Soldiers spent their winter months and times of peace in **forts**. A typical fort held between five hundred and one thousand troops. Every fort was defended by a ditch, a **rampart** and a high stone wall. In the center of each fort was the *principia* or headquarters of the fort. Here is a quote from Emperor Hadrian praising an army legion's wall-building skills:

*You have built a wall **entailing** long labor, such as is **customarily** made for permanent winter quarters ... built of large heavy stones of all sizes ... You have cut a trench straight through hard coarse gravel and have made it even by smoothing it.**

*Source: Excerpt, Hadrian's address to a legion in North Africa, A.D. 128.

See also: Creation of the Roman Empire 4–5, Rulers and Ruled 6–7, Travel and Trade 12–13, Buildings and Engineering 18–19

DEATH AND BURIAL

People in the Roman Empire did not have modern medicines, their diets were not very healthful, and their living conditions were extremely hard. The combination of these **factors** meant that many people did not live to reach the age of fifty. Many children died at birth or caught diseases that they could not fight off. The Romans were, therefore, very familiar with death. In fact, death was such a large part of their lives that they created all sorts of rituals for the **funeral** and burial of a loved one.

CEMETERIES

This ancient cemetery in Pompeii, Italy, is home to grand tombs that contain the remains of wealthy Romans.

In about 450 B.C., Roman law did not allow the dead to be buried inside the city walls. The law stated that:

*None is to bury or burn a corpse in the city.**

This ruling was made for religious reasons but also had a practical purpose, because it prevented the spread of disease in the tightly-packed streets of Roman towns. Cemeteries were built near town gates. The richest Romans were buried in **tombs** along the roadside. People who traveled on the road were able to see the tombs and remember those who were buried inside. Poorer people could pay for the ashes of their relatives to be placed in small spaces in special buildings. The bodies of the poorest members of Roman society and slaves were simply thrown together into large pits and buried without any funeral ceremony.

*Source: "Twelve Tables, Table X.1"

Word Discovery

afterlife *another world after death*

communal *used by members of*

a community or group

corpse *a dead body*

grieve *mourn deeply*

mourn *miss and remember someone who has died*

THE FUNERAL

Early in the Roman Empire, the **cremation** of a dead body was common. A **cinerary urn** was used to deposit the ashes of the **deceased**. The urn would then be placed in a family tomb or a cemetery. Romans later began to bury their dead. If there was enough money, a funeral took place within two days of a person's death, usually in the evening. A Roman writer commented about the funeral service for a rich man:

After this, when the burial and the usual rituals have been carried out, they place the image of the dead man in the most **conspicuous** *place in the house, enclosed in a wooded shrine. This image consists of a mask that reproduces his features and* **complexion** *with remarkable faithfulness.**

This Roman urn from the first century A.D. was made to hold the ashes of a young woman and honored her marriage.

*Source: Polybius, "Histories 53-4.3," second century B.C.

CASE STUDY

This coffin detail from about A.D. 150 to A.D. 180 shows the god Hercules at the gates of the underworld.

The River Styx

Throughout the period of the Roman Empire, there were many different ideas about death. Many people believed in an afterlife. Inscriptions on tombstones show that Romans believed that the dead would be ferried across the Styx, a river that led to the **underworld**. A coin was often placed in the dead person's mouth so that the ferryman could be paid. Here the process is described:

The ferryman there is Charon. Those sailing the waters of the Styx have all been buried. No man may be ferried from fearful bank to fearful bank of this roaring current until his bones are laid to rest.*

*Virgil, "Aeneid," late-first century B.C.

Glossary

cinerary urn container for storing dead person's ashes

complexion tone and texture of skin

conspicuous very obvious

cremation burning a dead body before burying or scattering the ashes

deceased a person who has recently died

factors things that actively contribute to a result

funeral observance held after someone's death

tombs structures where dead bodies are buried

underworld where the dead gather under the earth

See also: Rulers and Ruled 6–7, Religion 8–9, Travel and Trade 12–13, Health and Medicine 22–23

BUILDINGS AND ENGINEERING

The Romans copied many building styles from the Greeks, particularly large, important buildings, such as stadiums and temples. The Romans were the first to use domes on top of buildings. They were also the first to use many arches on their structures. Wherever the Romans built within their empire, they used local materials. For larger buildings, however, they brought in marble from Greece or Italy. The Romans were also the first to use concrete for building.

BUILDING TOOLS

Roman builders used drafting instruments called dividers to transfer measurements when they were working with models or drawings of the structure that they were building. If large blocks of stone had to be placed together on a building or a bridge, it was essential that the blocks fit together perfectly. The Romans used an instrument called a set square to make accurate angles. They also would have used a plumb bob to make sure that vertical lines were straight.

Good **engineering** depended on accurate measurements. The Romans unified measurements across the empire so that everybody knew how

to measure the length of something. The ruler is divided into the basic unit of length, the **digitus**. A digitus is about 0.7 inches (18.5 mm). There are 16 digiti in a pes and 5 pes in a passus. A Roman mile was about 1,000 passus in length.

This marble relief from the second century A.D. shows stonemasons at work.

Word Discovery

frontier *a border between countries or of a developed area*
irrigation *supplying water by*

man-made or artificial means
legacy *something passed on to people*

technology *way things work*
pozzolana *the Roman name for concrete*

CARRYING WATER

The Pont du Gard aqueduct in Nimes, southern France, built in the first century B.C.

The purpose of a Roman **aqueduct** was to provide a city with a water supply. The water would flow along the very top of a covered channel. Aqueducts show that the Romans did not build grand buildings simply to show off but that their structures also had a practical purpose. The importance of aqueducts to the water supply of Rome is described in the following quote:

*... they are structures of the greatest **magnitude**, and ... each one carries several **conduits**; for should it once be necessary to interrupt these, the City would be **deprived** of the greater part of its water supply.**

*Source: Frontinus, "The Water Supply of Rome II," late-first century A.D.

Glossary

aqueduct a structure for carrying large amounts of flowing water
conduits channels for water to flow through
deprived have something taken away
digitus the basic unit of measuring length in the Roman Empire

engineering the design of buildings, machines, products, and systems
forts army posts that may have high walls and towers
magnitude of great size or importance
marauding attacking and stealing

CASE STUDY

Hadrian's Wall

In A.D. 122, Emperor Hadrian ordered that a wall be built across northern England to mark the Roman Empire's border and to keep out **marauding** northern tribes. Modern historians think it took the army between six and eight years to build the wall and that it was over 75 miles (120 kms) long. Originally built of earth and wood, the wall was gradually converted to a stone wall about 33 feet (10 m) high and 7 to 10 feet (2 to 3 m) thick. This structure was made from local materials, such as rubble, mortar, and stone. To further increase the empire's defenses, **forts** were built every thousand paces along the wall's entire length. When completed, Hadrian's Wall was an impressive monument.

This is a view of Hadrian's Wall, which was built in northern England in the second century A.D.

See also: Travel and Trade 12–13, The Roman Army 14–15, Health and Medicine 22–23, Homes 28–29

GLADIATORS

A gladiatorial contest was a fight between two men (the *gladiators*) in front of a huge crowd, which only one man would survive. Today, people consider it the most barbaric of Roman customs, although in Roman times, these were very popular events. It is believed that gladiatorial contests began as part of a ceremony at the funerals of important people, such as warriors. By the time of the emperors, however, a fight between gladiators had simply become a spectacle for entertainment.

GLADIATOR FIGHTS

Gladiators were trained in special schools called **ludi**. They were often slaves and criminals, although many Romans actually chose to become gladiators.

If a gladiator survived many fights, he was regarded as a hero and might become famous. At the end of a fight, the crowd decided whether the loser should live or die. If the fight took place in front of the emperor, then the final decision was his. Roman statesman Pliny the Younger described the glory of being a gladiator:

*Next came a public entertainment – nothing **lax** or dissolute to weaken and destroy the manly spirit of his subjects, but one to inspire them to face honorable wounds and look scorn on death, be exhibiting love of glory and desire for victory.* *

This image of a gladiator comes from a mosaic made in the first century A.D. for an Italian Roman villa.

*Source: Pliny the Younger, "Panegyric," A.D. 100

Word Discovery

arena *enclosed area for entertainment or competition*
auditorium *part of a public*

building where audience sits
condemned *to be found guilty*
courageous *brave*

custom *usual practice*
glorify *strongly admire*
spectacle *a public display*

COLOSSEUM

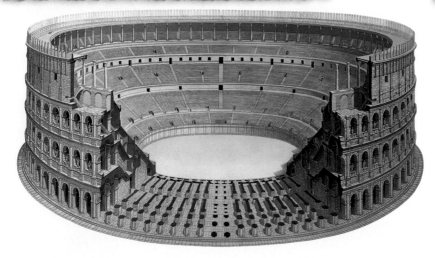

The Colosseum was used for fights between gladiators, animals, and people and animals.

The most spectacular place for gladiatorial contests was the Colosseum in Rome, which was completed in A.D. 80. It could hold over 50,000 people at one time. Enough of the Colosseum still stands to imagine what it first looked like. An **awning** could be stretched over the top to give shade to the crowd.

Below this were cells where the gladiators were held before being led out to fight. The arena they fought in was covered with sand, which would absorb the blood and be easily swept away. A Roman writer describes how:

*... at the dedication of the Colosseum, Titus provided a most **lavish** gladiatorial show.**

*Source: Suetonius, "Life of Titus, VII.3," first-half of the second century A.D.

Glossary

awning a rooflike cover over a place, often made of canvas
deflect turn aside from a straight path
exposed without shelter or protection
lavish fancy and expensive

lax not very firm or strict
ludi schools for training gladiators
retiarius a lightly armored gladiator
secutor a heavily armored gladiator
trident a spear with three points at the end

CASE STUDY

Gladiator's Gear

There were two types of gladiators — the **secutor** and the **retiarus**. The armor worn by a secutor gave some protection during the fight, but its weight could also slow the gladiator's movements. Meanwhile, a retiarus wore only a short tunic. This garment left him unprotected but made him much quicker. The retiarus also had a net that he used to try and catch his opponent and a **trident** with which to stab him. A Roman writer named Seneca describes a contest between two lightly armed gladiators:

*The men have no defensive armor. They are **exposed** to blows at all points, and no one ever strikes in vain ... there is no helmet or shield to **deflect** the weapon.**

Secutors would have worn helmets like this one from Pompeii, Italy, first century A.D.

*Source: Suetonius, "Life of Titus, VII.3," first-half of the second century A.D.

HEALTH AND MEDICINE

Many Romans believed that illnesses were caused by curses, witchcraft, or punishment from the gods. It was common for many people, therefore, to look to the **supernatural** for cures. Praying at shrines, carrying charms, and leaving offerings to the gods were all supposed to help cure an illness. Any medicines that were used were usually herbs with healing properties. Among the many cultural ideas that Romans adopted from the Greeks was their emphasis on cleanliness as an important part of good health.

ROMAN TOILETS

The Romans developed a water-supply system that helped prevent many diseases.

Toilets were **communal** and used as places to meet and talk with others. A stream of water flowed underneath the toilets and carried away waste. People would clean themselves with a sponge soaked in vinegar and on a stick. The vinegar would have killed any germs. The sponge was then cleaned in a small stream that ran in front of the toilets. Romans took great care of their sewers. In 33 B.C., Emperor Augustus' right-hand man and appointed heir, Agrippa:

*... cleaned out the sewers, and sailed underground through them to the Tiber.**

Roman toilets, such as these from Housesteads Fort on Hadrian's Wall, were built so that a stream of running water washed away any waste.

*Source: Cassius Dio, "History, 49.43.1-4," third century A.D.

Word Discovery

administer *give a remedy, such as a dose of medicine*
amputation *have a limb cut off*

grooming *taking care of one's appearance*
hygiene *habits of cleanliness*

that are good for health
sophisticated *highly developed*
talisman *a protective charm*

DOCTORS

Romans had no effective **anesthetics**, so any operation would have been a terribly painful experience. They did not have any **antiseptics** either, so wounds became infected, often leading to amputation or even death. Doctors tried to heal their patients with many different kinds of herbs, such as fenugreek for pneumonia and peppermint for stomach trouble. Emperor Marcus Aurelius had a doctor named Galen who wrote about a number of medical subjects:

> *About Marcus Aurelius I know personally that for his own safety he used to prepare and take each day as much as an Egyptian bean's worth (a small measure) of this **antidote**, swallowing this either with or without a mixture of water or wine or the like. And when he began to get very drowsy at his daily occupations, he took away the poppy-juice.**

A warrior named Aeneas has an arrowhead removed from his leg by a surgeon in this detail from a first century B.C. wall mural in Pompeii, Italy.

*Source: Galen, "On Antidotes 1.1," mid-second century A.D.

Glossary

anesthetics drugs given to numb pain before a medical procedure
antidote remedy to reverse effects of poison or disease
antiseptics mixture that kills germs
capacious roomy or with a lot of space

châtelaine a clasp to hold keys or a purse
communal used by members of a community or group
luxurious costly, of the best quality
supernatural caused by god or a spirit

CASE STUDY

This Roman châtelaine dates from the second century A.D.

KEEPING CLEAN

Most Romans visited the public baths to keep themselves clean. Lucian, a Roman satirist writing in the second century A.D., describes a **luxurious** bathing complex:

*... necessary for the reception of richer people ... **capacious** locker rooms to undress in on each side, with a very high and brilliantly lighted hall in between them, in which are three swimming pools of cold water; it is finished in Laconian marble ...*

Rich people often took their slaves to attend to their grooming needs. At other times, many Romans pinned a **châteleaine** of cleaning implements to their clothing. This might include tweezers, a nail cleaner, and an ear scoop.

*Source: Lucian, "The Bath," second century A.D.

See also: Death and Burial 16–17, Buildings and Engineering 18–19, Food and Drink 24–25, Leisure 30–31

FOOD AND DRINK

The Romans enjoyed food. Although they ate three meals daily, most people ate very little during the day and had their largest meal in the evening. Poor Romans ate a diet of mostly bread, lentils, and a small amount of meat. It was **fashionable** to add lots of herbs and spices to food for variety and because food was not always fresh. One of the most popular sauces made was a strong-tasting fish sauce called *garum*.

ROMAN COOKING

A central **hearth** was heated by burning wood or charcoal. Several emperors, including Julius Caesar, worried about the risk of fire in the cities, so they did not allow ovens to be used in people's homes.

Poorer Romans would not have been able to afford an oven even if they were allowed to have one. Instead, people bought hot meals from popular bars called *thermapholia,* which were found on many city streets. Roman writer Seneca describes these food vendors:

... the varied cries of the sausage dealer and **confectioner** *and of all the* **peddlers** *of the cook shops,* **hawking** *their wares, each with his own peculiar* **intonation**.*

Most cooking was done using saucepans made of bronze, because they cooked food more evenly than pots or pans made from other materials.

This stone oven is preserved in the city of Pompeii, Italy.

*Source: Seneca, "Moral Letter 41.2," mid-first century A.D.

Word Discovery

banquet *feast*
condiment *something used for flavoring food*

culinary *having to do with kitchens or cooking*
dilute *weaken flavor or strength*

by adding something else
etiquette *polite behavior*
indulged *enjoyed or satisfied*

DRINKS

Wealthy Romans drank from glass drinking cups, while ordinary Romans used pottery cups. Most people drank wine. It was considered bad manners, however, to drink wine without first adding water to it. Romans also flavored their wine with herbs and honey. In a letter, Pliny the Younger describes how a dinner host gave different qualities of wine to his guests:

He had even put the wine into tiny little flasks, divided into three categories, not with the idea of giving his guests the opportunity of choosing, but to make it impossible for them to refuse what they were given. One lot was intended for himself and for us, another for his lesser friends (all his friends are graded) and the third for his and our freedmen.

Wealthy Romans would have used this glass drinking vessel from the fourth century B.C.

*Source: Seneca, "Moral Letter 41.2," mid-first century A.D.

Glossary

confectioner person who sells sweets
fashionable in style at the time
Gaul modern-day France
hawking selling goods by calling to customers in the streets
hearth the areas of a fireplace or over a fire where things can be heated

intonation the rise and fall of the voice when speaking
peddlers salesmen
unique the only one; without equal
vessel a hollowed utensil used for holding something

CASE STUDY

Samian ware plates, such as this one from the third century A.D., were very popular in ancient Rome.

BOWLS AND PLATES

Rich Romans wanted to eat their meals off of the most fashionable bowls and plates available. In the first and second centuries A.D., a glossy red pottery called Samian ware would have been the first choice of most fashion-conscious Romans. Samian ware was made in large factories in Italy and **Gaul** and was shipped to every corner of the Roman Empire and beyond. First-century writer Petronius mocked a rich man who boasted about the quality of his plates and glasses:

*Perhaps you're wondering why I am **unique** in owning Corinthian plates? Because, of course, the dealer I buy it from is named Corinthus.*

*Source: Pliny the Younger, "Letters, II.6," early-second century A.D.

See also: Travel and Trade 12–13, Death & Burial 16–17, Health & Medicine 22–23, Homes 28–29

CLOTHES AND JEWELRY

The Romans cared about the clothes they wore and made sure that they also had the best jewelry, hairstyles, and makeup. Children did not have fashions of their own but simply wore smaller versions of their parents' clothing. Styles changed throughout the period of the Roman Empire. In the early years of the empire, for example, Roman men had long hair and curly beards. By the end of the empire, however, it was fashionable to be clean-shaven and to have short hair.

THE CLOTHES THEY WORE

All Roman citizens had the right to wear a **toga,** but this garment was only worn on special occasions. On other days, both men and women wore light **tunics**. They wore sandals, too.

Both togas and tunics were large, single pieces of cloth that were fastened at the shoulder with a brooch or a pin. Light colors, especially white, were popular. Trousers were seen as only fit to be worn by barbarians and foreigners. In fact, one sign of the influence of Roman ideas on the territories that were conquered by the empire was if the people in those lands adopted the Roman style of dress. Tacitus, in his account of his father-in-law Agricola's governorship of Britain, records that:

...even our style of dress came in to favor and the toga was everywhere to be seen [in Britain].*

This funerary mosaic from the first century B.C. shows a man wearing a white toga.

*Source: Tacitus, "Agricola 21," A.D. 97-98

Word Discovery

appearance *the way someone or something looks*
cosmetic *makeup; related to appearance or making beautiful*
fashionable *stylish*
pendant *a piece of jewelry worn on a necklace*
sandals *shoes made of a sole fastened to the feet with straps*

ROMAN JEWELRY

Women wore a lot of jewelry. Romans originally followed the Greek example of setting gemstones into rings and bracelets. The Romans then took this idea further by adding different kinds of stones and pearls. Both men and women wore rings, sometimes on all ten fingers. The wealthiest Romans also wore **cameos** set into rings and pendants. A cameo normally pictured people, gods, or mythological figures. Poet Juvenal, who didn't like women very much, wrote about the way that women dressed up in jewelry:

> *There is nothing that a woman will not permit herself to do, nothing that she deems shameful, when she encircles her neck with green emeralds, and fastens huge pearls to her **elongated** ears: there is nothing more **intolerable** than a wealthy woman.**

This pure gold amulet from the first century A.D. was found in Pompeii, Italy.

*Source: Juvenal, "Satir VI," late-first to early-second century A.D.

Glossary

cameos small pictures carved from one material that are placed on top of another material
complexion tone and texture of skin
elongated stretched
funerary mosaic artwork made to honor someone who has died

intolerable unbearable
ocher a red or yellow mineral made of clay
sediment material that settles at the bottom of liquid
toga loose flowing piece of outer clothing
tunics slip-on clothing that is belted, sleeveless, and knee-length

CASE STUDY

This small makeup grinder from the first century A.D. was found by a metal detector in Britain.

Makeup Grinder

Makeup grinders were used to crush minerals into a powder to use as makeup. Rich Roman women wore makeup whenever they were going out in public. It was fashionable to have a pale **complexion**. Looking pale showed that a woman did not have to go outdoors to work. Many women applied makeup to make themselves look even paler. This type of makeup was normally made of chalk or white lead, which was very poisonous. Cheeks and lips were colored red using **ocher** or the **sediment** from red wine. Eyebrows and the edges of eyes were normally tinted black with ash. Makeup was kept in small pots and bottles.

See also: Creation of the Empire 4–5, Language and Writing 10–11, Travel and Trade 12–13, Gladiators 20–21

HOMES

Most Roman homes were small and of low quality. In towns and cities, people lived in crowded **tenements**. These buildings were several stories high and had no running water or **sanitation**. More is known about houses in cities than about those in the country. We know, for example, that several emperors worried about the condition of the tenements and passed laws to limit their height. Wealthy Romans could afford both a town house and a country **villa**.

ROMAN HOUSES

Wealthy Roman landowners lived in houses called *villas*. Most Roman villas had the same design. The first room that a visitor would walk into would be the entry hall, or ***atrium***. The atrium had an opening in the roof and a pool. The opening helped to keep the house cool in summer, and the pool collected rainwater.

Frescoes from the Roman period show that rooms contained little furniture but that Romans liked rich decorations on their walls and floors. In other parts of the Roman Empire, the style of villas varied and copied local designs. Early villas in Britain were usually a row of rooms with a **colonnade** across the front. In a letter to a friend, the younger Pliny boasted of "the charm of [his] Laurentine villa" in Italy, saying that:

*... the villa is spacious enough for my needs, and the upkeep is not expensive.**

This is a view from the outside of a Roman villa in Herculaneum, Italy.

*Source: Pliny the Younger, letter to a friend, late-first to early-second century A.D.

Word Discovery

architecture *practice of designing and building structures*
decor *interior decorations*

design *creative arrangement*
landscape *pictures of the outdoors; outdoor plantings*

legend *traditional story*
residence *home*
thermal *related to heating*

DECORATING THE HOUSE

The homes of wealthy Romans had floors decorated with **mosaics**. This form of decoration was practiced in Egypt in the third century B.C. and was adopted by the Romans. Many mosaics have survived because they were very strong once their tiles were set in place. The scenes on mosaics were usually taken from legends or daily life. In addition to their beautiful floors, villas often had walls decorated with frescoes. These paintings were usually scenes out of Greek mythology. Wealthy Romans also had outdoor scenes painted on the walls, so that they looked like views out a window.

This wall mosaic of a man drinking is from the first century A.D. Villa mosaics often showed scenes from daily life.

Glossary

atrium central hall of a Roman villa
colonnade spaced line of columns, usually supporting a roof
frescoes paintings done on walls while the plaster is still wet
hypocaust an early system of under-floor central heating

mosaics decorations created by fitting small pieces of tile together to form pictures or patterns
sanitation relating to the disposal of waste and sewage
tenements poor apartment buildings
villa house of a wealthy Roman

CASE STUDY

This hypocaust from the first century B.C. is from the Gallo-Roman town of Alesia in France.

Keeping Warm

Villas in the northern parts of the Roman Empire needed to be heated. To do this, people used a central heating system under the floor called a **hypocaust**. A fire was lit next to an outside wall and was kept going by a slave. The heat would be drawn into an open space underneath the floor and would then rise through the floor into the walls. In some villas, the heat passed through holes in the wall as well. These hypocausts can be seen in many Roman buildings, particularly in Pompeii, Italy. Pliny describes the use of a heating system to keep his villa warm:

*Attached to this is a bedroom connected to a passageway with a hollow floor and walls fitted with pipes from which it receives hot air circulated in all directions at a healthful temperature.**

*Source: Pliny, "Letter, II. 17," late-first to early-second century A.D.

See also: Religion 8–9, Buildings and Engineering 18–19, Food and Drink 24–25, Leisure 30–31

LEISURE

Every Roman, except for slaves, was given many holidays. Originally, these were days that celebrated religious festivals. Over time, however, the activities that went with these festivals lost their religious meaning and became just entertainment. In the reign of Emperor Claudius, 159 days a year were declared as public holidays. By the middle of the fifth century A.D., this total had risen to two hundred holidays a year. Enjoying **leisure** time was an important part of Roman life.

THEATER

Many Roman towns had an open-air theater. These were usually **semicircular** in shape.

The audience sat on the curved sides of the theater facing a raised stage. The plays that were performed were either Greek plays that had been translated into Latin or plays that were written by Romans in the Greek style. Roman theatergoers liked comedies best. The Romans also invented two new forms of theater. They were the first people to use **mime** and **pantomime**. The importance of theater and entertainment is illustrated by the following quote from an early Roman writer:

... it was the height of political wisdom for the emperor not to neglect even actors and other performers of the stage, circus and the arena, since he knew that the Roman people is held fast by two things above all, the grain supply and the theatrical shows.*

This mosaic of a tragic theater mask was created in the first century A.D.

Source: Fronto, "Elements of History, XVII," early-to-mid-second century A.D.

Word Discovery

corruption improper actions done in return for money or personal gain
festivities fun celebrations
performance acting or playing music
patron person who supports the arts or an activity
popular liked by many people
vulgar not pleasant

PUBLIC BATHS

The public baths, such as this one in the English city of Bath, were popular places to spend leisure time.

The Romans went to the public baths not only to keep clean but also to meet friends, exercise with weights, or play ball games. For people with less energy, there were board games, throwing dice, and marbles. Roman writer Seneca, who lived above some baths, paints a clear picture of the public baths:

When the stronger fellows are exercising and swinging heavy laden weights in their hands, when they are working hard or pretending to be working hard, I hear their groans ... Add to this the arrest of a brawler or a thief, and the fellow who always likes to hear his own voice in the bath, and those who jump into the pool with a mighty splash as they strike the water.*

*Source: Seneca, "Moral Letter 41.1-2," mid-first century A.D.

Glossary

corruption acting dishonestly for money or personal gain
dregs most undesirable parts
fraction part of a whole
leisure time free from work that can be spent on fun
lingo foreign language
lyre popular stringed instrument that was plucked like a harp
mime acting with gestures and actions but no words
pantomime piece of drama or poetry with music and dance
semicircular shaped like half of a circle

See also: Language and Writing 10-11, Health and Medicine 22-23, Food and Drink 24-25

CASE STUDY

The God of Music

According to Roman mythology, the god Apollo would entertain the other gods with music and poetry. For this reason, Apollo was seen as the patron god of music. Wealthy Romans thought music was something that was beneath them. The Roman writer Juvenal even complained that listening or dancing to music could lead to **corruption,** largely because these activities were associated with Greek luxury. As Juvenal says:

*I cannot abide a Rome of Greeks; and yet what **fraction** of our **dregs** comes from Greece? The Syrian Orontes has long since poured into the Tiber, bringing with it its **lingo** and its manners, its flutes and its slanting harp-strings.**

Music was popular with most people, however. Musical instruments included the **lyre** and many types of wind instruments.

This second century A.D. statue of the Roman god of music, Apollo, is from Cyrene, Libya.

*Source: Juvenal, "Satire III. 58," late-first–early second century A.D.

INDEX

TIME LINE OF ANCIENT ROME

753 B.C.
The city of Rome is founded by Romulus and Remus (according to Roman mythology).

509 B.C.
The Republic of Rome is established after the Etruscans are driven out.

450 B.C.
The Romans establish their first written laws called the Twelve Tables.

390 B.C.
The Gauls invade Italy and are defeated by the Romans.

300-400 B.C.
The Romans are exposed to Greek ideas. They begin to worship Greek gods and goddesses, but they give them Roman names.

197 B.C.
Rome conquers Spain.

140s B.C.
Rome gains control of North Africa, Greece, Macedonia, and part of Turkey.

First Century B.C.
Rome conquers eastern Asia Minor, Syria, and Judea under the direction of general Pompey.

58-51 B.C.
Julius Caesar conquers Gaul (modern France).

49 B.C.
Caesar invades Italy, starting a civil war.

44 B.C.
Caesar is assassinated by a group of Senators who hope to restore

the Roman Republic. Civil war breaks out again.

43 B.C.
Mark Antony fights for control of Rome, seeking help from Cleopatra, queen of Egypt. They fall in love.

30 B.C.
Rome conquers Egypt.

27 B.C.
Augustus becomes the first emperor of Rome. His rule marks the period known as Pax Romana (Roman Peace). It lasted for about 200 years.

A.D. 30
Jesus Christ is crucified by the Romans for treason. However, his followers begin to spread Christianity throughout the Roman Empire.

43 Emperor Claudius invades Britain

200s
The Goths, a Germanic tribe, invade the Roman Empire on numerous occasions.

Late 300s
Christianity becomes the official religion of the empire.

Early 400s
Germanic tribes invade Spain, Gaul (now France), and northern Africa

410
The Visigoths invade and loot Rome.

476
The last Roman emperor is overthrown.